MIA
HAMM

BY RICHARD RAMBECK

GRAPHIC DESIGN
Robert A. Honey, Seattle

PHOTO RESEARCH
James R. Rothaus, James R. Rothaus & Associates

ELECTRONIC PRE-PRESS PRODUCTION
Robert E. Bonaker, Graphic Design & Consulting Co.

PHOTOGRAPHY
Cover photo by Associated Press AP
Photo spread on pages 2 & 3 by Allsport

Library of Congress Cataloging-in-Publication Data
Rambeck, Richard
Mia Hamm / by Richard Rambeck
p. cm.
Summary: A breif biography of the accomplished athlete who was named top female player by the U.S. Soccer Federation three years in a row.
ISBN 1-56766-523-3 (library : reinforced : alk. paper)

1. Hamm, Mia, 1972- — Juvenile literature.
2. Soccer players—United States—Biography—Juvenile literature.
[1. Hamm, Mia, 1972- 2. Women soccer players. 3. Soccer players. 4. Women—Biography] I. Title
GV942.7.H27R36 1998   97-42443
796.334'092 — dc21   CIP
[B]   AC

CONTENTS

Hamm is controlling the ball against China in 1996.

As much as her ankle hurt, Mia Hamm knew she was going to play. She had to play. After all, this was the game for the gold medal at the 1996 Olympics. The winner, either the United States or China, would become the first nation to claim an Olympic gold medal in women's soccer. The 1996 Summer Games in Atlanta marked the first time women's soccer was an Olympic event. Hamm and her U.S. teammates had vowed to win the gold in front of the home fans. And there were *lots* of fans: 76,481 people were in the stands of Sanford Stadium in Athens, Georgia, for the gold medal game.

LARGEST CROWD EVER

It was the largest crowd ever to see a women's soccer match. The fans had come to see the top teams and players in the world. The United States had won the first women's World Cup, in 1991. The U.S. finished third in the second World

7

Cup, in 1995, losing to Norway in the semifinals. The American team and Norway were the co–favorites to win the 1996 Olympic gold medal. Hamm was one of the main reasons the U.S. was expected to do so well. The quick, talented forward was one of the best players in the world. In fact, Hamm was chosen to be the U.S. Soccer Federation's Female Athlete of the Year in both 1994 and 1995.

United States beat Norway 2-1 in 1995.

PLAYING HURT

Unfortunately, Hamm had not been at full speed for most of the Olympic tournament. She suffered a bad ankle sprain in the team's second game, a 2–1 victory over Sweden. The injury was so bad, U.S. Coach Tony DiCicco decided to keep her out of the next game. Without Hamm, the U.S. tied China 0–0. The tie could have been costly for the American team. It meant that the U.S., and not China, would have to face the powerful

Hamm with trophy after defeating Norway in 1995.

Norwegians in the semifinals. Norway, which won the 1995 women's World Cup championship, was a tough, physical team. Hamm played in the game, but she was not at her best.

THE FINALS

The U.S. and Norway played to a 1–1 tie, forcing sudden death overtime. Then, nine minutes into overtime, Shannon MacMillan scored the game–winning goal. The U.S. was in the finals and would face China, a 3–2 victor over Brazil in the other semifinal game. This time the Chinese would have to deal with Hamm, but she was still not at 100 percent. Her ankle was still very sore. There was, however, no question that Hamm would play. "I was not going to miss this game for anything," she said. Injured ankle and all, Hamm proved to be a problem for China's defense.

A DANGEROUS PLAYER

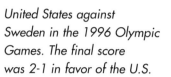

United States against Sweden in the 1996 Olympic Games. The final score was 2-1 in favor of the U.S.

In the 18th minute of the match, Hamm got loose in the penalty area, firing a well–placed shot at China's goal. Chinese goalkeeper Zhong Honglian dove and got one hand on the bullet from Hamm, deflecting the shot. However, the ball went right to MacMillan, who scored the first goal of the match. The huge crowd went wild, screaming for several minutes. The goal was a big lift for the U.S.—and for Hamm. She didn't score the goal, but her shot created the chance for MacMillan to put the Americans on top. It also showed the Chinese that Hamm was still a dangerous player.

ONE FINAL TRICK

Later, China tied the game, but Hamm and the U.S. had one final trick up their sleeves. In the 68th minute, Hamm made a pass that set up a two–on–one break for the U.S. As the crowd roared, Tiffeny Milbrett scored the goal that proved to be the winner. In the final minutes of the

Hamm's pledge of allegiance after defeating South Korea 6-1 in 1997.

match, Hamm re-injured her ankle. She had to be carried off the field on a stretcher. Seconds later the match ended, and the celebration began. Hamm might have been hurt, but she had no trouble walking to the medals stand to receive her gold.

A TEAM EFFORT

"I would have loved to have been 100 percent [during the Olympics], but I wouldn't trade this win or how we played in this tournament for anything," Hamm said. "From the beginning, this has been an entire team effort. Everyone involved came up big. It wasn't just offense. Our defense was awesome." It was, truly, a team effort. MacMillan and Milbrett weren't considered stars, but they scored the most important goals of the tournament. Hamm's Olympics involved more bravery than brilliant play. "Mia was incredible," said midfielder Trish Venturini. "I don't know how she kept going."

NOT YET A STAR

Hamm holding nephew, Dillan Hamm.

Mia Hamm has been going for a long time on the soccer field. Only 24 years old when the U.S. won the Olympic gold medal, she had been playing on the national team for nine years. Hamm was only 15 when she made her national team debut in August 1987. Four years later, she helped lead the U.S to the championship in the first World Cup. She started five of the six games in the Cup and scored two goals. Back then she was a midfielder, not a forward, and she was the youngest member of the U.S. team. While she was a good player, she wasn't yet a star. That would change.

AN EARLY BEGINNING

Mia Hamm began playing soccer when she was five years old. "I played because my older brother and sisters played," said Hamm, who is one of six children. "And my father was a coach and referee." Hamm was born in Selma, Alabama, in

Hamm playing for the U.S National Team, the Rochester Ravens.

1972. Her family moved around a lot before settling in Virginia. By the time she was in high school, Hamm was already one of the top female soccer players of any age. In 1987, she joined a U.S. national team coached by Anson Dorrance, also the coach at the University of North Carolina.

COLLEGE YEARS

Hamm scored her first goal for the national team in 1990. That same year she joined Dorrance at North Carolina. In college, Hamm became the all–time leading scorer in NCAA women's soccer history! In 91 games for North Carolina, Hamm scored 103 goals and added 72 assists. She also led the Tar Heels to four NCAA titles. Hamm was voted national college player of the year three times. Meanwhile, she was also becoming a star on the national team. "We've watched her mature into one of the best players in the world," said U.S. forward Carin Gabarra.

A MODEST LEADER

Her U.S. teammates may have thought she was one of the top players in the world, but Hamm didn't. She knew the U.S. team was loaded with great talent. "I know I'm not," Hamm said about being the best in the world. "I train with these players every day. That's what's nice, when you're surrounded with great players. Every practice is a humbling experience. It's like, wow, I wish I could do that." Hamm had become a leader on the team, but she was a quiet one. "I don't say a lot before the game," she said. "I don't say a lot in general."

→

Hamm in action against Australia. The U.S. won 2-1 in 1996.

TOP FEMALE PLAYER

Hamm was named the U.S. Soccer Federation's top female player in 1996, the third straight year she received the honor. In 1996, she led the U.S. national team with 18 assists and was second with nine goals. "There are three athletes who have brought their sports

20

Hamm shows desire during a game with Portugal.

to a new level," said Phil Knight, chairman of Nike. "Michael Jordan in basketball, Tiger Woods in golf, and Mia Hamm with women's soccer." In 1999, Hamm will try to lead the U.S. to its second World Cup title. This time the tournament will be held in the United States. She and her teammates expect nothing less than another championship.